FERVENTLY INTENSE

UPGRADING YOUR SPIRITUAL ARSENAL FOR VICTORIOUS PRAYERS

LATISHA SHEARER

Fervently Intense
Upgrading Your Spiritual Arsenal For Victorious Prayers
Published by ForWord Books
21143 Hawthorne Blvd, Ste 184
Torrance, CA 90503

Scripture quotations are taken or paraphrased from several versions of The Holy Bible.

ISBN 979-8-9882642-5-5

Copyright © 2023 by Latisha Shearer

All rights reserved. No part of this book may be reproduced or transmitted in any form or by any means, electronic or mechanical, including recording and photocopying, or by any information storage and retrieval system, without written permission from the publisher.

Published in the United States by ForWord Books

FERVENTLY INTENSE

DEDICATIONS

To my cherished grandmother, Katherine Jefferson,

You, a faithful prayer warrior, have shown me the beauty of unrestrained communion with God. Through your example, I learned that prayers aren't confined by time or form; they're conversations that flow from the depths of the heart. You boldly approached the throne of God, unapologetically pouring out your soul, teaching me the transformative power of fervent, extended prayers. This book, "Fervently Intense," stands as a tribute to your legacy and an embodiment of the fearless prayer warrior you are.

To my dear friend and brother, Anthony Thigpen,

Your perceptive insight and prophetic vision have left an indelible mark on my path. Who could have foreseen that those stacks of prayer journals, once confined to the corners of my room, would evolve into the pages of best-selling books? Your words, spoken in simple sincerity, breathed life into a dream I scarcely dared to acknowledge. "Fervently Intense" is a realization of that vision—an embodiment of the journey we've shared, a testament to your faith in me, and a celebration of the profound impact you've had on my life.

Latisha Shearer

ACKNOWLEDGMENTS

Embarking on the journey to write "Fervently Intense" was a leap into the unknown, a step beyond the boundaries of my comfort zone. I once believed I couldn't write an entire book alone, but this experience has been both challenging and incredibly humbling. While I've contributed to anthologies before, this solo endeavor has been a profound test of my dedication and determination.

First and foremost, I want to express my gratitude to my dear friend, Sandra Reese. Your unwavering support and encouragement played a pivotal role in bringing it to fruition. Just when I began to doubt, your belief in the concept renewed my resolve. Thank you for holding me accountable, Sandra.

Apostle Janice Grier, your sermon spoke directly to my heart, validating the essence of this book in ways beyond explanation. Your timely words fortified my resolve and rekindled my commitment to this project.

To my beloved spouse, Shaun Shearer, and my wonderful children, Makiya and DeVonte Shearer, your unwavering belief in me sustained me through the long hours and challenging moments. Your sacrifice of time and understanding allowed me to pour my heart and soul into these pages, and for that, I'm forever grateful.

I sincerely appreciate the support and guidance provided by Apostle Mike Ebron, Dr. Crystal Witherspoon-Jackson, Latia Hereford, and Suzanne Hambrick. Your unyielding support, willingness to lift me when I stumbled, and commitment to ensuring I remained focused and consistent in fulfilling what God called me to have been invaluable. Thank you for being pillars of strength and encouragement throughout this process.

FERVENTLY INTENSE

I've found the unwavering support, encouragement, and belief in each of you that made this book possible. I am eternally grateful for your presence in my life, and I look forward to the impact "Fervently Intense" will have on the world, knowing that your contributions have shaped it in immeasurable ways.

With heartfelt gratitude,

Latisha Shearer

FERVENTLY INTENSE

TABLE OF CONTENTS

FORWARD
viii

PREFACE
x

CHAPTER ONE
**NOT AGAINST FLESH AND BLOOD:
UNVEILING THE UNSEEN BATTLES**

1

CHAPTER TWO
**UNLEASHING POWER THROUGH PRAYER:
THE FERVENT CONNECTION**

7

CHAPTER THREE
**DIVINE WARRIORS IN ACTIONS:
ANGELIC FORCES UNVEILED**

15

CHAPTER FOUR
**BEYOND SWORDS AND SHIELDS:
ARSENAL UPGRADE**

24

FORWARD

Prayer is a powerful weapon used to enhance the lives of born-again believers. However, prayer is communication with God; the more advanced your prayer language is, the more assets you have at your disposal. In the Bible, Matthew Chapter 17 describes a spiritual battle with unclean spirits in which the disciples struggled to get rid of the spirit. They asked Jesus why this spirit didn't come out like the rest, and Jesus responded, "Howbeit this kind goeth not out but by prayer and fasting" (Matthew 17:21 KJV). Here, we have biblical proof that prayer can grant us victory. In the book of Genesis Chapter 21, after years of being barren, through prayer, Sarah, in old age, was able to bring forth a son for Abraham. Displaying more biblical proof that prayer can grant us victory in areas where we feel defeated. Heaven's army is righteously awaiting our command when we understand the rules of engagement on the battlefield.

An excerpt from part one of this book provides you with more insight and details on how to understand and upgrade your prayer language. "As weaponry has evolved in the natural realm, so has it progressed in the spiritual dimension. The concept of supernatural beings imparting knowledge to humanity finds resonance in various cultural narratives. In the Book of Enoch, Azael, also known as Azazel, is said to have taught humans the craft of metalworking, a revelation that transformed technological advancement. This parallel resonates with the biblical account of Tubal-Cain, who delved into the art of forging with metals like bronze and iron (Genesis 4:20-22). Both figures stand as envoys of progress, ushering humankind into an era of innovation fueled by the mastery of metals. Their intervention highlights the extraordinary

FERVENTLY INTENSE

leaps made possible when divine knowledge intersects with human ingenuity." Commander Prophetess Latisha Shearer provides high-level intelligence during part one of the book, which serves as the Operation Order, providing you with the spiritual situation, our mission as believers when engaged in prayer, and the execution of how to fulfill our mission. When we pray, we don't pray amidst; we have an intended target, and we will never surrender, retreat, or accept defeat. The operation order also includes logistics and methods of communication.

Prophetess Latisha Shearer is an anointed General of prayer, equipping the body of Christ aggressively in mastering the art and skill of intercession on the earth. She's a wife and mother but also a beloved daughter of God called to bring elevation to the kingdom structures in the earthly realm. Prophetess Shearer mirrors the blueprint between the governmental armies and the army of the Lord. This two-part book will challenge every believer to grow deeper in intimacy with the Lord and even push unbelievers to understand the language of prayer, inviting them into a relationship with Christ and ultimately leading them to salvation. As an Apostle who trains, equips, and develops intercessors globally around the world in thirty-eight states and five countries, I stand in agreement with Prophetess Shearer, the commander of the intercessory movement known as "Fervently Intense." These strategies and resources will go down in history as the spiritual prayer boot camp and training ground of Heavenly communication being re-established on the earth.

Apostle Mike Ebron Jr

PREFACE

In a world trapped by the dazzling allure of the material, where the noise of daily life often drowns out the whispers of the unseen, "Fervently Intense" emerges as a radiant beacon, a clarion call, and a meticulously crafted manual. It extends its hand to believers, inviting them to ascend the ladder of spiritual consciousness, sharpen their focus, and elevate their prayers of spiritual warfare to an unprecedented intensity. Within the pages of this literary masterpiece, a transformative journey awaits, ushering readers into a realm that lies beyond the veil of the visible, where the ceaseless battle between light and darkness unfolds on a plane that evades the grasp of the naked eye. This battleground, stretching far beyond the physical confines, calls for a wholehearted immersion—a commitment to engage with unyielding intention and enthusiasm.

As the words of Ephesians 6:12 resound, they take on the cadence of a timeless battle cry, echoing across generations: "For we do not wrestle against flesh and blood, but against principalities, against powers, against the rulers of the darkness of this age, against spiritual hosts of wickedness in the heavenly places." Within the intricate fabric of existence, believers discover themselves unwittingly entangled in this celestial conflict, where their souls and spirits become interwoven in a profound struggle that extends beyond the observable and reaches into the depths of spiritual essence.

"Fervently Intense" is a rich composition crafted with a revelation of our divine purpose and a guiding force that leads us through the complex passages of spiritual conflict. It presents us with a pivotal inquiry that demands introspection and exploration: Are the prayers we offer for spiritual warfare truly effective, possessing the potency required to dismantle the intricate schemes masterminded by the adversary? As you turn each page, you'll hear a call, encouraging you to plunge into the depths of your prayer life, peel away the layers of routine supplication, and uncover the reservoir of power that courses through your spiritual connections.

No longer are we relegated to timidity or a sense of inadequacy in our approach to the spiritual battlefront. This confrontation we enter defies the confines of the ordinary, the realm of the physical, and the transient nature of time. Within the intricate design of "Fervently Intense," you'll discover a profound revelation: the realization that genuine effectiveness lies in the earnest and powerful prayers of the righteous (James 5:16b). The call reverberates through these pages, urging believers to transcend the realm of mediocrity and embrace the extraordinary intensity demanded by the domain of spiritual warfare.

While journeying through the sacred realms within the Bible, we witness the emergence of celestial armies and divine commanders, taking on the roles of central figures in the hidden accounts of spiritual warfare. The angels' multifaceted roles and strategic precision are discussed as they guide us through the complexities of our spiritual battles. Yet, as we reflect upon these age-old clashes, we uncover a truth—a revelation—that our spiritual arsenal must evolve, just as human weaponry and tactics have transformed over time.

"Fervently Intense" stands not merely as a book but as an open invitation—an invitation to ascend to a higher plane of engagement, a summons to wield the transformative power of fervent prayer within the uncharted terrain of spiritual warfare. It is an appeal to embrace our roles as spiritual warriors with unwavering determination, acknowledging that the battles we wage extend beyond mere visibility. With hearts ablaze and spirits fortified, the moment beckons to intensify our prayers, amplify our resolve, and step boldly onto the battlefield of spiritual warfare, armed not only with the timeless wisdom of ages past but also with the contemporary strategies that resonate with the complexities of our time. Through the revelation and prayers of "Fervently Intense," believers are called to be a force that can neither be ignored nor silenced—a force that stands unshaken, fervently intense.

CHAPTER ONE

NOT AGAINST FLESH AND BLOOD: UNVEILING THE UNSEEN BATTLES

Engaging in spiritual warfare thrusts us into a realm unseen by the naked eye, a battleground that extends beyond the physical into the spiritual. As believers, we're firmly rooted in the conviction that this spiritual realm is not a mere abstract concept but a living reality. However, though many acknowledge its existence, it often remains shrouded in indifference, seldom earning a second thought. The scriptures bear the coexistence of virtuous and evil forces within this realm. What escapes our notice is the veiled battle waged right within our own domains, unfolding in living rooms and bedrooms. Our perception often fails to pierce the veil of the natural, the realm we can tangibly sense, leaving us prone to addressing matters solely from a worldly perspective.

Navigating the spiritual realm with sensitivity mandates more than acknowledging its presence; it necessitates keen awareness and vigilance. Much like the tangible world, the spiritual sphere embodies a parallel dynamic of good and evil. On the side of righteousness, the spiritual side, we often encounter the divine – God (Father, Son, and Holy Spirit) and angelic messengers. These heavenly messengers are divine agents dispatched to aid us in our struggles. In opposition, the opposite spectrum comprises malevolent entities: Satan, his demonic cohorts, and the cloak of darkness that enshrouds them. Among these are demons, once angels of light, who forfeited their divine stature to follow the path of rebellion paved by Satan. Their endeavor remains consistent – to thwart and annihilate God's design, ceaselessly ensnaring us through deception and temptation.

FERVENTLY INTENSE

When God dispatches His divine messengers, it's to uplift and nurture us, as beautifully affirmed in Hebrews 1:14. In striking contrast, when Satan dispatches his agents, it's a sinister attempt to afflict and destabilize, as aptly articulated in 1 Corinthians 12:7. This ceaseless clash of virtue and vice constitutes a perpetual undercurrent, casting its influence across every facet of our existence. As we glance into the arena of spiritual warfare, let's begin to cultivate a fervent consciousness of the unseen realm and the ceaseless tussle that shapes our lives.

Venturing into the heart of the spiritual realm unveils a dynamic interplay that defies our natural perceptions. It's a stage where the timeless battle between good and evil finds its battleground. In this ethereal domain, the forces of darkness relentlessly labor to impede and obliterate God's divine plans. Conversely, the forces of righteousness zealously strive to orchestrate the realization of God's purpose here on earth. This spiritual warfare, a truth intrinsic to every Christian's journey, isn't a mere theological abstraction; it's an undeniable facet demanding our attentive recognition and steadfast readiness. As believers, we find ourselves thrust into this spiritual skirmish whether we consciously acknowledge it or not. Ephesians 6:12 resounds in our ears, reminding us, "For we do not wrestle against flesh and blood, but against principalities, against powers, against the rulers of the darkness of this age, against spiritual hosts of wickedness in the heavenly places."

One might ponder puzzling terms like principalities, powers, rulers, and spiritual wickedness. What lies beneath these veiled titles? Who or what embodies these names? These are shepherds for the devil, with a mission to carry out the nefarious intentions of Satan himself. Though intangible to our physical senses, their presence and influence within the natural realm carry undeniable potency and authenticity.

FERVENTLY INTENSE

Exploring the realm of spiritual warfare, we encounter a term that holds profound significance — "principalities." This term pertains to entities wielding dominion and power over specific territories or groups of people. In spiritual warfare, "principalities" denotes a distinct class of spirits vested with authority over particular regions or communities. This authority extends to influencing and affecting those within their sphere of influence.

The narrative of principalities finds resonance in the pages of Scripture. Take, for instance, the book of Daniel, where the figure of the Prince of Persia emerges. This principality reigned over the vast dominion of the Persian Empire. Scripture indicates that this spirit tried to obstruct an angelic messenger's mission to convey a revelation to Daniel, requiring the intervention of the archangel Michael to halt the hindrance orchestrated by the Prince of Persia. The principalities' objective is to obstruct God's purpose and hamper the progress of His followers. We must stay armed and ready, equipped to face the forthcoming battle, bolstering our faith as we persistently and continuously overcome these adversarial forces.

Another entity we encounter is "powers." Powers wield authority over specific aspects of our lives, orchestrating attacks against believers to impede their spiritual advancement. These powers are skilled at deploying tactics like sickness, poverty, and addiction to undermine our growth and journey of faith.

Sickness is one of their most prevalent strategies used to deprive believers of their well-being and vitality. It manifests through physical ailments and mental distress, exerting a substantial toll on our spiritual progress. Amid sickness, maintaining fervent prayer and engaging in spiritual practices becomes difficult, and our faith can waver under the weight of pain and adversity. The powers also employ poverty as a potent weapon to assail believers. Instilling financial hardship impedes our ability to exhibit generosity, support our loved ones, and heed God's call upon our lives. The burden of poverty amplifies stress and anxiety, further obstructing our spiritual growth and impact. Addiction emerges as another cunning maneuver employed by these powers. They cunningly ensnare believers in destructive behavioral cycles, whether substance abuse, pornography, or other vices. This enslavement thwarts our spiritual progression, trapping us in self-destructive patterns and obstructing our pursuit of God's purpose.

In all these instances, the powers execute their designs relentlessly, aiming to hinder our spiritual trajectory. They strive to strip us of health, prosperity, and freedom, seeking to deter us from embracing God's divine plan. As believers, it's imperative that we discern these calculated attacks and actively engage in spiritual warfare to overcome them. Armed with the knowledge of their tactics, we stand equipped to confront these challenges head-on and reclaim the spiritual ground that is rightfully ours.

However, "rulers of the darkness of this world" takes on profound meaning. It serves as a vivid descriptor for the spiritual forces orchestrating our world's intricate systems and structures. These systems encompass governments, media, education, and other influential institutions that intricately mold societal beliefs and values. Anchored beyond the visible, these rulers are spiritual entities operating behind the scenes, relentlessly influencing the trajectory of human affairs.

In the Bible, we find vivid illustrations of these rulers at play. The New Testament casts light on the "rulers of this age," instrumental in the tragic crucifixion of Jesus Christ. These spiritual forces relentlessly endeavor to sculpt and dominate the world's landscape, enforcing their distinct agenda. Indeed, the grip of these rulers is palpable across numerous facets of our society.

FERVENTLY INTENSE

The media, a potent influence, shapes our cultural convictions and worldviews. Television, cinema, and social platforms sway public sentiment, weaving a fabric of prevailing ideology. The government's sway extends through laws and policies that structure our existence. As another conduit, education molds societal convictions through teachings on history, science, and diverse subjects.

For believers, cultivating awareness of these potent forces is paramount, driving us to engage in spiritual warfare with unyielding determination. We summon the powerful artillery of prayer, fasting, and the indomitable strength of the Holy Spirit. As we navigate these currents, discernment must reign supreme regarding messages emanating from the media, the government, and other institutions. We tread cautiously, refusing to succumb to their agendas. Ultimately, we find solace in the sovereignty of God over these rulers of the world's darkness. As believers, we stand assured that God's dominion prevails and that His kingdom will triumph over the rulers of this age. Armed with unwavering faith, we withstand opposition, persistent in the omnipotent power of God to defeat the rulers of darkness that seek to subvert His divine purpose.

The realm of spiritual warfare unveils another intriguing facet — "spiritual wickedness in high places." This term signifies the most influential and formidable demonic spirits, which wield their influence within the spiritual sphere to manipulate and sway those occupying positions of authority or leadership. These spirits are ethereal forces relentless in their pursuit of control and manipulation over those who wield societal power and influence. These spiritual entities craftily work to bend those in positions of authority to their evil agenda. The manifestations of this spiritual wickedness in high places are diverse — from corruption, deceit, and insatiable greed to oppressive acts, injustice, and violent upheavals. They thrive by sowing seeds of division and discord and undermining the values that uphold peace, justice, and equality.

For us as believers, it's paramount to prevent the influence wielded by spiritual wickedness in high places and to engage fervently in spiritual warfare to overcome their grip. A discerning eye towards messages emanating from authoritative figures is essential, coupled with a steadfast determination to resist their influence. Ultimately, we draw solace from the truth that spiritual wickedness in high places is subject to God's dominion. As believers, we find comfort in the undeniable reality that God is the ultimate authority, and His kingdom will ultimately triumph over the forces of darkness. This assurance empowers us to stand firm in our faith, even in the face of opposition, trusting in the omnipotent power of God to conquer spiritual wickedness in high places.

That said, the question arises: Why engage in spiritual warfare? The answer is simple—we're in an ongoing battle. The sinister forces led by Satan and his demons are resolved to thwart our realization of God's purpose and the abundant blessings He intends for us. These demonic entities seek to rob us of life's essence, as their very aim is to "steal, kill, and destroy," as stated in John 10:10. Their relentless tactics limit our spiritual growth and impede our progress. That's precisely why we must wholeheartedly embrace spiritual warfare, standing unwaveringly against the severe onslaughts of the adversary.

CHAPTER TWO

UNLEASHING POWER THROUGH PRAYER: THE FERVENT CONNECTION

The pages of Revelation unveil a glimpse into realms beyond the natural, where an intense spiritual battle rages. Amid these verses, an epic struggle ensues between the forces of light and the forces of darkness. The power of God emerges as the triumphant force and crushes Satan and his cohort, ultimately establishing the supremacy of God's kingdom over the shadows of malevolence. Amidst our daily routines, the adversary prowls, seeking whom he may ensnare, as Peter's words echo in 1 Peter 5:8, "Stay alert! Watch out for your great enemy, the devil. He prowls around like a roaring lion, looking for someone to devour."

Diving into Peter's warning of alertness and awareness, the distinction becomes pronounced. To be alert means to be watchful and vigilant – like a vigilant guard standing watch. On the other hand, awareness pertains to recognizing and comprehending one's surroundings. Judges 7:5-7 illustrate this as Gideon's warriors are divided. Some, cupping water to their mouths, remain watchful, while others kneel, their awareness lacking against swift ambushes.

This interplay isn't limited to ancient accounts; it resonates within our own narratives. In life's skirmishes and conflicts, God's promise takes shape – a divine army musters to shield us in the spiritual realm. Recall the moment the King of Aram mobilized his forces to ensnare Elisha in Dothan's grip. Firm in faith, Elisha reassured his anxious servant, declaring, "Don't be afraid... Those who are with us are more than those who are with them." As Elisha beseeched

God to unveil the unseen, the servant's eyes opened, revealing divine chariots ablaze with fire surrounding them.

The need for action becomes apparent after exploring the significance of being alert and aware. Psalm 24:8 resonates here as it declares boldly, "Who is the King of Glory? The strong and mighty, the Lord mighty in battle (Jehovah-Gibbor Milchamah)." When the battles against principalities, powers, and unseen entities arise, Jehovah Gibbor takes action on our behalf. We, as sons and daughters of the Almighty, find our confidence in the Lord mighty in battle. In this truth, we can mirror Jesus' approach by praying to our Abba Father, instantly summoning more than 60,000 warring angels to stand by us.

Peter found it challenging to maintain alertness and intercede for Jesus (Mark 14:32-42). So, by the time the Roman soldier came to apprehend Jesus, Peter was attempting to confront a spiritual conflict through physical means. In this passage, Peter unknowingly does not follow Jesus' spiritual lead. Engagement on the battlefield had already commenced in the spiritual realm, making initial contact and manifesting in the natural before Peter attempted to intervene. Jesus' response: "Put your sword back in its place... Do you think I cannot call on my Father, and he will at once put more than twelve legions of angels at my disposal?" This reference to "legions" refers to Roman military units, symbolizing great strength. Jesus conveys that His Father, Jehovah Gibbor, could have readily deployed over 12 x 6,000 warring angels, totaling a minimum of 72,000. This notion reminds me of the account in Isaiah 37:36, where a single angel vanquished 185,000 men in a single night. These divine warriors would have rallied to Jesus' aid, demonstrating their unwavering allegiance to His cause.

While Jesus didn't call upon the aid of 72,000 legions of angels, He disclosed a hidden truth – we have the privilege to actively seek our

Father's intervention, and angels will be dispatched on our behalf. This revelation presents the question: Are we petitioning our Heavenly Father to send forth more than 72,000 angels to engage in the battles that impact our health, relationships, finances, children, businesses, thoughts, marriages, ministries, communities, and areas of influence?

Engaging in spiritual warfare demands a proactive approach and an offensive stance against the adversary's schemes. Jesus, with His deep discernment, had already identified the spirit that had entered Judas, anticipating an imminent attack. Instead of being caught off guard – a situation many of us find ourselves in – Jesus moved into an offensive prayer stance, not merely reacting defensively but attacking through prayer. It was in prayer that He found peace in the midst of the brewing storm. Jesus could have invoked angelic armies, seeking heavenly reinforcements. Worth mentioning is the zeal with which Jesus waged spiritual warfare. Our prayers cannot remain confined to brief intervals of 5 to 10 minutes if we seek victory in battle. Jesus demonstrated strategic fervency, spending hours in prayer. Such persistence is essential as we entreat divine intervention to thwart attacks on our divine purpose.

It is crucial to recognize that our spiritual adversaries, the principalities, powers, rulers of darkness, and spiritual hosts of wickedness, are unmoved by mere displays of emotion – tears, raised voices, or passionate supplication. The lesson gleaned from the Bible is clear: the effectual, fervent prayers of the righteous avail much (James 5:16b). We must ask ourselves: Are our prayers for spiritual warfare genuinely effective? Are they potent enough to counteract the schemes of the enemy seeking to disrupt our path?

The life of Daniel stands as a testament to the power of prayer. A man deeply committed to communion with God, often fasting and praying on behalf of Israel. One fateful day, Daniel received a profound vision from God, revealing the unseen battle that raged over his beloved nation. Through this vision, he witnessed an angel locked in combat against an evil spiritual prince who ruled the Persian Empire. In this struggle, the angel disclosed to Daniel that the prince of Persia hindered his arrival, yet Michael, the archangel, came to his aid. This event offers insight into the intricate dynamics of spiritual warfare and how it relates to our earnest prayers.

In Chapter 10 of Daniel, we encounter a prophetic revelation that brought Daniel great sorrow. Much like our responses to unwelcome news today, his heart sank. The impending message foreshadowed a period of intense persecution and trial for Israel. Grieving and concerned, Daniel embarked on a three-week period of mourning and fasting, highly aware of the challenges ahead. During this time, he became aware of a spiritual presence in the room – an encounter similar to Paul's experience on the road to Damascus in Acts 9:3-9.

As the being clothed in linen appeared, Daniel and those in his company experienced terror and awe, even though they couldn't fully discern the presence. Similar to instances in our lives when divine interactions might be sensed by some but not fully grasped or sensed by others today. Daniel was instructed to stand and informed, "For I have now been sent to you." This notion of being "sent" underscores the spiritual assignment of this angelic messenger. Furthermore, the being explained that from the very first day Daniel began to pray, his words were heard and prompted the angelic visitation. Are our words aligning with divine intervention or conceding to fear, despair, and defeat? Sometimes, we feel overwhelmed, uttering a simple plea like "Lord, have mercy." One of the best pieces of advice I ever received from my mother is, "Lord, have mercy, is prayer." Sometimes, that is all we can utter. While such moments are understandable, they might diminish in frequency if we adopt an offensive, rather than defensive, posture in prayer.

Our prayers become most potent when they are characterized by fervency when we roar in spiritual battle instead of worrying and "woe it's me" prayer styles. Returning to Daniel, we determine that his prayers caused the angel's dispatch. However, it encountered resistance – a spiritual struggle against the prince of the kingdom of Persia that spanned twenty-one days. This opposition indicates the evil nature of this prince, for it sought to thwart the reception and understanding of God's prophetic message. This concept parallels with principalities within the angelic hierarchy detailed in Ephesians 1:21, 6:12, Colossians 1:16, and 2:15, as well as references to Satan as the prince of this world (John 12:31, 4:30, and 16:11).

Ultimately, the encounter with Daniel illustrates the necessity of persistent, offensive prayer, even in the face of opposition. Just as Daniel's prayers moved the heavens, our prayers possess the potential to break through spiritual resistance, ushering in God's intervention in our lives and the world around us.

As believers, we often find ourselves falling into the trap of praying earnestly about a specific matter for a few days, only to become disheartened by the absence of immediate results, assuming that God's answer must be a resounding "no." It's a pattern we've likely all experienced – we seek an answer, and when it doesn't manifest quickly, we question whether our prayers have been heard. What if the reason for the delay is not a rejection but a spiritual battle that requires our enduring persistence? Enter Daniel, an exemplar of such endurance. For twenty-one days, he maintained an unwavering posture of prayer, denying his own needs and comfort to engage in spiritual warfare. His steadfast dedication bore fruit in the form of a supernatural encounter.

Daniel's encounter indicates that our breakthroughs, blessings, miracles, and healings may be delayed in the unseen realm, requiring us to push forward persistently. Whether the waiting period is a single day, eleven, twenty-one, forty-one, sixty-one, or even one hundred and one days, the message is clear: Do not give up.

While Daniel's exact words of prayer remain unrecorded, it's unlikely that he spent his prayer time bemoaning his circumstances or questioning God's silence. Instead, he was likely engaged in fervent, intense, and focused spiritual warfare. Think about the fiery fans or coaches of combat sports like boxing or UFC. They're not passive bystanders; they're on their feet, passionately shouting strategic advice. Some even mirror the fighters' motions in the air, embodying the battle themselves. When watching football, my husband and I often find ourselves trying to push the pile of players to gain that extra yard or prevent the yard needed for a first down or touchdown point. In the spiritual realm, powerful demonstrations like these wield significant impact. For instance, I know an apostle who physically wields a sword during her prayers as a prophetic demonstration of her spiritual combat against bondages and obstacles.

In my own experience, the Holy Spirit communicates spiritual warfare in the language I readily understand, a language surrounding my military background. Similarly, others find unique ways to engage, each suited to their understanding. Whether a prophetic gesture or a symbolic weapon, these actions are emblematic of the spiritual authority we possess as believers. Of course, we don't physically engage in these battles; we are not in full armor alongside them on the battlefield.

FERVENTLY INTENSE

One thing for sure is that our words in prayer hold incredible power. Through them, we can pre-emptively dismantle spiritual strongholds, preventing their manifestation in the physical world. Our words can transform the trajectory of our lives, signaling to the heavenly realm that we are ready for angelic reinforcements to wage war on our behalf. Today, we stand on the precipice of our next level of elevation, prepared to speak words of intensity and authority that shake the enemy's camp and draw the attention of heaven's angelic forces. Our prayers are not cries of defeat but battle cries of victory.

The battles we face in the spiritual realm are not a game of chance like paper, rock, or scissors. There's no time for playful gestures when we're up against adversaries who are relentless in their pursuit to kill, steal, and destroy every aspect of our lives. Their aim is clear: to obstruct, deter, or entirely thwart God's plans and purposes for us. Such was the intensity of the spiritual warfare in Daniel's circumstance – combat so formidable that even Michael, one of the chief princes, had to assist the divine being. Yet, this holy warrior did not rest for long; the battle continued, with the prince of Persia requiring another engagement. Moreover, the prince of Greece loomed on the horizon, preparing for the next confrontation.

Ephesians 6:12 speaks of principalities, describing them as the rule of princes. These are not flesh-and-blood rulers but spiritual entities that exert authority over nations. When Michael, the archangel, is called "your prince," it's directed singularly toward the Prince of Israel, Daniel's people. The prince of Persia and Greece sought Israel's voluntary submission, desiring dominion over their chosen people. In the supernatural realm, these principalities are elevated in rank and dedicated to the affairs of nations like Persia and Greece. Denying their existence is to discount their powerful influence over nations and their destiny.

FERVENTLY INTENSE

As there are principalities over significant nations, there are also those assigned to regions and individuals. The works of these principalities make praying for governmental authorities essential. Rulers of darkness at this level wage attacks to maintain a stranglehold on nations and perpetuate conflicts. Though you may not be a government leader, the decisions at that level trickle down, affecting every facet of life; even those considered to be the most minor interactions eventually show up. And just as there are demonic influences on a nation, there are those assigned to specific states, counties, cities, neighborhoods, and even family bloodlines.

While I can't describe what the warfare between the messenger of God and the prince of Persia resembled precisely, I am sure it entailed the usage of the weaponry of that age. As a combat veteran, I can attest that modern-day militaries no longer engage in combat with iron swords and arrows; our methods have evolved. Similarly, spiritual warfare has taken on different forms over time. It's perplexing why some persist in using arrows as weaponry of choice when engaging in spiritual battles when you can use something more long-range, such as a guided missile. Our warfare is not merely a battle of the past; it's ongoing, evolving, and dynamic. Let's equip ourselves with the contemporary strategies and spiritual weaponry needed to overcome the principalities and powers that oppose us. Our fight is not against flesh and blood but against spiritual forces that require our modern, fervent, and focused engagement.

CHAPTER THREE

DIVINE WARRIORS IN ACTIONS: ANGELIC FORCES UNVEILED

David, renowned as both a warrior and a skilled soldier, was no stranger to battle. Numerous conflicts marked his life, each contributing to his mastery of warfare's language and tactics. This profound comprehension often found its way into his prayers, where he employed combat vocabulary to address his adversaries. Psalm 35:1-3 (NIV) presents one such instance where David adorns his plea to God with military terminology: "Contend, Lord, with those who contend with me; fight against those who fight against me. Take up shield and armor; arise and come to my aid—Brandish spear and javelin against those who pursue me. Say to me, 'I am your salvation.'" In these verses, David skillfully weaves warfare imagery to articulate his desperate need for divine intervention and safeguarding from his enemies. He implores God to "contend" with those who stand against him, evoking the sight of a battle-ready warrior prepared to engage. The imagery deepens as he beseeches God to "take up shield and armor," invoking the visual of a guardian readying for combat. This prayer is David's heartfelt plea for God's direct involvement in his circumstances, a request bolstered by the powerful language of warfare.

David was acutely aware of the spiritual climate of his era, understanding the influence of the rulers of darkness within his time. In the present, we must release David like prayers against our adversaries; however, we must not limit our spiritual warfare to the ancient usage of arrows in our prayer language. We face adversaries who are the rulers of darkness in this age, a formidable opposition extending to other periods beyond our time. It's crucial to elevate our spiritual strategy beyond limited approaches. David's prayers were fervent, heartfelt, and strategic, a testament to his understanding of the complexities of the spiritual realm. As modern believers, we too can draw from David's example, recognizing the need for both fervor and sophistication in our spiritual warfare. Just as David's prayers were not confined to a single method, we must embrace a holistic approach to engage the spiritual forces that oppose us. Let us be as skillful as David, employing the entire arsenal during prayer, also aligned with discernment, wisdom, and faith to overcome the rulers of darkness in every age.

As weaponry has evolved in the natural realm, so has it progressed in the spiritual dimension. The Book of Enoch contains the concept of supernatural beings imparting knowledge to humanity. Azael, also known as Azazel, is credited with teaching humans the craft of metalworking, a revelation that significantly advanced technology. This parallel resonates with the biblical account of Tubal-Cain, who delved into the art of forging with metals like bronze and iron (Genesis 4:20-22). Both figures stand as envoys of progress, ushering humankind into an era of innovation fueled by the mastery of metals. Their intervention highlights the extraordinary leaps made possible when divine knowledge intersects with human ingenuity.

The spiritual and earthly domains exchange isn't confined to the past. In our contemporary world, the idea of waging war with swords, arrows, and horses may seem feeble when set against today's technology — from Gatling guns to drones. While angels are perceived as having insights beyond human understanding, their teachings, as exemplified by Azazel, can veer towards unrighteousness. It is a stark reminder that the influences of the spiritual realm can extend into modern weaponry, shaping the violence we encounter and steering individuals toward modern

FERVENTLY INTENSE

semi-automatic assault weapons instead of archaic arms.

Like that displayed in Daniel 10, prophetic foresight attests to the angelic engagement in present battles that herald future outcomes. In a world where ancient swords and spears cannot adequately represent the instruments of war, prophetic insights emerge as potent predictors of impending events. The divine realm's strategic involvement isn't confined to historical eras but continues to shape the course of humanity's journey. Today, as we navigate our existence amidst an intricate interplay of spiritual forces, let us embrace the present realities. Our warfare encompasses the complexities of our time, extending beyond antiquated weaponry. Just as divine beings play a part in shaping our world's destiny, our prayers and actions remain crucial in this ongoing struggle. As history unfolds, the battles we face may differ from those of old, but the unyielding importance of vigilance, discernment, and prayer remains steadfast.

Navigating the battles of today, it's crucial to recognize that some of our struggles are interwoven with the fulfillment of our future aspirations. When I mention "tomorrow," I'm referring to where you envision yourself next year, three years, or even five to ten years. Each level of achievement is intricately linked to your purpose. While it's tempting to indulge in creature comforts and social media distractions, we're all here for a more profound reason. Just as the angel stood ready for what lay ahead, we must remain vigilant. Often, right after a victory, a new challenge emerges. Instead of fixating on tomorrow's skirmishes, let's direct our energy toward securing our destiny and the destiny of our families, businesses, and health in the years to come. Many of us are still shaping a five-year plan and waging a determined battle to see it come to fruition. The saying goes, "Plant seeds today that your future self will harvest with gratitude." Have you ever felt that you're walking in the answer to prayers from days gone by? Our thoughts become words; words become actions; actions form habits; habits shape character; character molds destiny. Knowing this, we must ensure that our words are not obstructions, hindering the natural manifestation of our future.

A profound insight into the nature of our warfare is unveiled in 2 Corinthians 10:3-6: "For though we live in the world, we do not wage war as the world does. The weapons we fight with are not the weapons of the world. On the contrary, they have the divine power to demolish strongholds. We demolish arguments and every pretension that sets itself up against the knowledge of God, and we take captive every thought to make it obedient to Christ. And we will be ready to punish every act of disobedience once your obedience is complete." In these verses, the apostle Paul sheds light on the essence of spiritual warfare and the strategies believers employ to advance the gospel and uphold Christian principles. Paul underscores that while we reside in the physical realm, our battles transcend worldly methodologies. The "weapons of the world" signify human strategies, whereas "divine power" encompasses the spiritual arsenal accessible to us through Christ. These spiritual resources have the potency to dismantle strongholds, which may manifest as false beliefs, sinful behaviors, or any opposition to God's truth. The focus is directed at confronting spiritual barriers and forces rather than physical confrontations. We often overlook the fact that we're entrenched in a cosmic struggle between good and evil. Although we lack material weapons like swords and guns, our words possess the capacity to trigger such weaponry in the spiritual realm. Our battles extend beyond the surface, encompassing the spiritual, the temporal, and the eternal. The evolution of weaponry mirrors the dynamic shifts in the spiritual realm, culminating in the realization that our words are potent agents of change in this divine struggle. As we wage war, let us draw upon our spiritual resources, affirming our destiny, dismantling strongholds, and embracing the profound connection between our words and our future.

Consider Daniel's context: his fervent prayers ignited a spiritual struggle that unveiled the "prince of Persia" as a formidable opposing force. This adversary sought to counteract the prophetic message that foretold the Persian Empire's fall and the rise of Greece. In today's world, Iran, the descendant of Persia, still harbors ambitions concerning Israel's fate. Could the same malevolent mission continue, now channeled through Iran's leadership? This narrative underscores the persistent nature of spiritual opposition. Like the "prince of Persia," our adversary remains resolute in its aims. This reality necessitates prayers that match the intensity of extreme force. Just as Daniel's prayers encountered resistance, our prayers must be unyielding and potent, capable of thwarting adversarial agendas.

This understanding fundamentally transforms our approach to prayer. We should never feel ashamed for praying with overwhelming force, recognizing that our battle isn't against mere flesh and blood. Our spiritual warfare isn't waged against governmental authorities, employers, acquaintances, or even loved ones. Instead, our contention lies with spiritual entities working through or influencing these individuals. To emerge triumphant, we must grasp the nature of our opponent, for failure could result in devastation across emotional, financial, relational, physical, and spiritual dimensions. Throughout the Bible, angels consistently embody powerful beings. They function as both God's messengers and His warriors, organized into armies with appointed leaders who guide them in battles against the forces of darkness. These angelic armies and their commanders play pivotal roles in the spiritual warfare that unfolds across the biblical narrative. The angels within God's armies undertake diverse roles and responsibilities in spiritual warfare. While their specific functions may vary depending on the circumstances, angels fulfill specific general roles in these divine battles. Here are a few illustrative examples:

Protection - An essential function of angels within God's armies is safeguarding believers. Psalm 91:11-12 affirms, "For he will command his angels concerning you to guard you in all your ways; they will lift you up in their hands so that you will not strike your foot against a stone." These verses underscore the role of angels in shielding and preserving God's people from harm.

Revelation - Angels also serve as divine messengers who unveil God's will and intentions to humanity. The apostle John writes in Revelation 1:1 that the book of Revelation was "sent and signified by his angel to his servant John." Throughout the book of Revelation, angels appear before John, unveiling the forthcoming events.

Deliverance - Angels in God's armies play a role in liberating believers from danger and oppression. Acts 12 recounts an angel's appearance to Peter in prison, leading him to freedom by breaking his chains. Hebrews 1:14 describes angels as "ministering spirits sent to serve those who will inherit salvation."

Judgment - Angels also execute God's judgments against the forces of darkness. In Revelation 9:15, angels are depicted as being "prepared for this hour and day and month and year" to carry out God's judgment against His enemies. In Revelation 16, angels pour out the bowls of God's wrath upon the earth, bringing judgment and destruction to those who oppose God's purpose.

Incorporating these insights into our understanding of spiritual warfare empowers us to wield potent prayers and navigate the battles with strategic awareness. Just as angels actively engage in this cosmic conflict, so too can our fervent prayers initiate powerful transformations in both the spiritual and natural realms.

FERVENTLY INTENSE

These are merely glimpses of angels' multifaceted roles within God's armies. Each role is intricate and purposeful, collaborating harmoniously to fulfill God's intentions in the spiritual realm. As believers, we can find solace in the knowledge that we possess formidable allies in these angelic armies, tirelessly laboring on our behalf to safeguard, steer, and liberate us in our spiritual conflicts. The book of Revelation unveils yet another striking illustration of angel armies. In Revelation 19:11-16, John's vision unfolds as Jesus rides a white horse, accompanied by armies on white horses. These divine forces are adorned in "fine linen, white and clean," marching alongside Jesus to battle against the dominions of darkness. The angel commanders outlined in the Bible further enhance our understanding of spiritual warfare. We already established this in examining the account of Daniel 10; we encounter an angel commander dispatched to aid the prophet, Daniel. The angel reveals that God sent him to respond to Daniel's prayers but encountered resistance from the "prince of the kingdom of Persia." This prince isn't a terrestrial ruler but a spiritual entity opposing God's designs.

Jude, too, alludes to angel commanders, labeling them as "archangels." In Jude 1:9, the text recounts a confrontation between the archangel Michael and the devil. Michael courageously rebukes the devil, declaring, "The Lord rebuke you!" The deployment of angel armies and their commanders in spiritual warfare underscores God's dominion and supremacy over the forces of darkness. These divine entities surpass mere messengers or aides; they are mighty warriors embroiled in fierce combat against the adversaries of God's realm. Guided by influential and potent angel commanders, these armies exemplify God's prevailing might and His unwavering authority.

As we navigate our own spiritual battles, we can draw inspiration from these angelic armies. They serve as a reminder that our God is not passive but actively engaged in the ongoing struggle between light and darkness. With heavenly forces at His command, we, too, can approach our battles with courage, knowing that we are part of a supernatural conflict where God's sovereignty prevails. As Generals in prayer, we can command the angelic commanders to lead their troops with authority, faith, determination, and confidence that the ultimate victory belongs to the Almighty.

The Bible intricately weaves angels on the battlegrounds of spiritual warfare. These divine entities, organized into armies and led by commanders, underscore the supremacy of God's authority over the forces of darkness. Their presence unveils the profound reality that our battles transcend the physical realm, deep into the spiritual expanse. We are surrounded by the vigorous might of God's angelic hosts. However, I wonder if these divine assemblies, often referred to as "Angel Armies," even encompass specialized divisions, like an "Angel Airforce" or "Divine Marines"?

The divine assemblies can choreograph attacks by airways, water, or land, engaging in spiritual battle wherever warranted. It paints a vibrant picture of angelic forces converging to counter the encroaching shadows, aligning with divine purpose. The Bible's accounts of these divine warriors participating in crucial historical moments, especially in the battles mentioned in the Old Testament, are hardly missed. Their interventions signal pivotal shifts between light and darkness, good and evil. From guarding believers to executing divine judgments, angels are indeed significant players in this cosmic battle.

Angelic commanders emerge as prototypes of authority harmonized with service. These leaders reflect God's might while orchestrating His plans. The angel who confronted Daniel or the archangel Michael engaging in divine confrontations exemplifies their roles within this divine hierarchy. This divine choreography extends beyond ancient texts; it resonates in our modern spiritual journeys. It serves as a reminder that we are not alone as we grapple with personal battles, uncertainties, and challenges. Angel armies stand as unwavering sentinels, embodying God's promise of protection, guidance, and deliverance. Much like earthly military units uniting for strength, these Divine warriors stand as a united force guided by a higher purpose.

Considering the notion of specialized angelic divisions—a Divine Airforce or Marines—invokes intriguing speculation. While Scripture doesn't explicitly detail such distinctions, it offers glimpses into the richness and diversity of angelic roles. These speculative analogies remind us of the intricacies of the divine realm, woven with threads of purpose and service. Our appreciation for these heavenly companions may deepen on our spiritual journey as we contemplate these divine arrangements.

CHAPTER FOUR
BEYOND SWORDS AND SHIELDS: ARSENAL UPGRADE

One of the most intriguing contrasts between modern military prowess and the weapons depicted in the Bible is the stark divergence in precision and accuracy. Within biblical accounts, soldiers launched arrows toward adversaries without the finesse of modern targeting systems, though still accurate. The evolution of military tactics and technology from the Old Testament to today's era stands as a testament to human ingenuity and innovation. Our current arsenal consists of guided missiles, fortified tanks, unmanned drones, orbiting satellites, and the list goes on, entities unimaginable to our ancient counterparts. This chasm in technological progression casts a spotlight on the profound metamorphosis warfare has undergone across the epochs. Guided missiles now navigate with surgical precision, minimizing collateral damage and optimizing effectiveness.

Another substantial variance surfaces in the velocity and mobility of contemporary military forces. Scriptures depict armies trekking on foot or horseback, constrained by limited mobility. In our present reality, machinery and aircraft grant swift traversal over vast distances, ensuring rapid deployment and agile responses to emergent situations. The cadence of warfare has quickened, enabling forces to flex across nations swiftly and decisively.

Within the modern military landscape, specialization carves the path forward. Branches like the Marines, Air Force, Navy, and Coast Guard unite collectively, each wielding unique competencies and mandates. This harmonized division optimizes proficiency and amplifies the overall impact in combat scenarios. Remarkably, while these advancements and distinctions stand in stark contrast, the core principles of strategy and tactics remain resolute. Whether it's ancient chronicles or contemporary conflicts, the art of warfare hinges on strategic intelligence, tactical skill, and adaptability to fluid circumstances.

As humanity's tools and tactics have evolved, the echoes of ancient wisdom endure. In both eras, the essence of conflict calls for discernment and inventive thinking. A profound shift in strategy or tactics often serves as the pivot of victory. It is a testament to the enduring nature of human challenges that our approach to overcoming them remains, in essence, unchanged. Wisdom remains the guiding star, transcending the ages and nations of war.

The Bible resonates with the resounding call to adapt strategies and tactics in the face of adversaries. Tales from Scripture echo this principle, like the Israelites' encirclement of Jericho's walls and David's triumphant slaying of Goliath. While modern military strategies and weaponry have undergone a revolutionary metamorphosis since the days of the Old Testament, the bedrock principles of strategy and tactics endure. Success hinges on the compass of wisdom and discernment, interwoven with creative thinking and adaptability to shifting landscapes.

In conclusion, as you embark on a journey of fervent and intense spiritual warfare prayers, it's imperative to grasp a foundational truth: achieving a balance between spiritual warfare prayers and worship and praise holds profound significance. As wise generals discern the opportune intervals for combat and retreat, you must also recognize when to step into the battle, emerge as a conqueror, and come off the battlefield and rest. Ponder the sobering reality that some warriors bear the hidden scars of battles deep within, their minds echoing the ceaseless turmoil of warfare. There is no exemption for battle fatigue for those in physical and spiritual battles who find it hard to disengage.

Allow me a momentary deviation to emphasize that even seers and prophets can find themselves confined within psychiatric walls due to the absence of skill in disengaging from the unrelenting conflict. Thus, I urge you to embrace intervals of worship and praise. Let your spirit resound with affirmations, commanding the very essence of your next level. Prophecy over yourself – it's akin to binding a battle wound with an expertly applied dressing. This act serves as a healing balm for the wounds incurred in life's skirmishes.

However, unleash your prayers with heightened intensity in the moments designated for warfare. Unleash fervent supplications without relenting, standing steadfast until you've defeated your adversary. The call to pray rings around us, an invitation to fortify ourselves at the intersection of supplication and spiritual elevation. In this realm, our words take on their own life, forging pathways of victory and igniting angelic interventions. Let us embark on this journey of prayer with unswerving faith and relentless determination, knowing that we are part of an unending divine battle armed with the might of heaven itself.

John 1:1 In the beginning was the Word...

A CHRISTIAN BOOK PUBLISHING COMPANY

We would be honored to publish your book!

CONTACT US VIA EMAIL AT
FORWORDBOOKS@GMAIL.COM

Made in the USA
Las Vegas, NV
21 December 2023